Loss, Grief and Hope

Aisha Ahmed

BookLeaf Publishing

Presentation by *BookLeaf Publishing*

Web: www.bookleafpub.com

E-mail: info@bookleafpub.com

ISBN: 9789357745239

First edition 2023

Dedicated to our sweet angel

We miss you so much

Gone but never forgotten

*Lots of love from Mummy, Daddy and
Sumaya*

ACKNOWLEDGEMENT

I would like to thank my husband Asim for being my rock through this hard time and my daughter Sumaya for being my sunshine. I am so blessed to have both of you and I love you so much!

PREFACE

I have been writing poetry since I was a little girl and I love poetry so much. I get inspired by many things like love, family and life. Words come to me and I turn them into poetry.

I recently suffered a miscarriage and I have been really upset dealing with my loss. It was my husband Asim who suggested me to write a poem on our loss as I have a passion for poetry and so I did, before I knew it I ended up writing many poems and I ended up with a series of poems.

From the heart, these words of mine are spoken truly from deep within and released into the outside world. As I was writing these poems I had tears coming out and emotional moments but I'm glad to have found somewhere to let these words be free.

Close to my heart and close to you, here is my Loss, Hope and Grief

Broken Dreams

A road of broken dreams is what laid ahead, knowing that you won't be here in my arms. My heart aches of sadness, my arms remain empty. I crave your presence but you choose to go to a better place. Not a day goes by without you on my mind, gone but never forgotten.

Twinkle Toes

The excitement building up until the two lines appear, the wait is over. A brand new chapter, a brand new journey. Tears of joy and happiness, a glow of radiance. Another pair of twinkle toes are on their way.

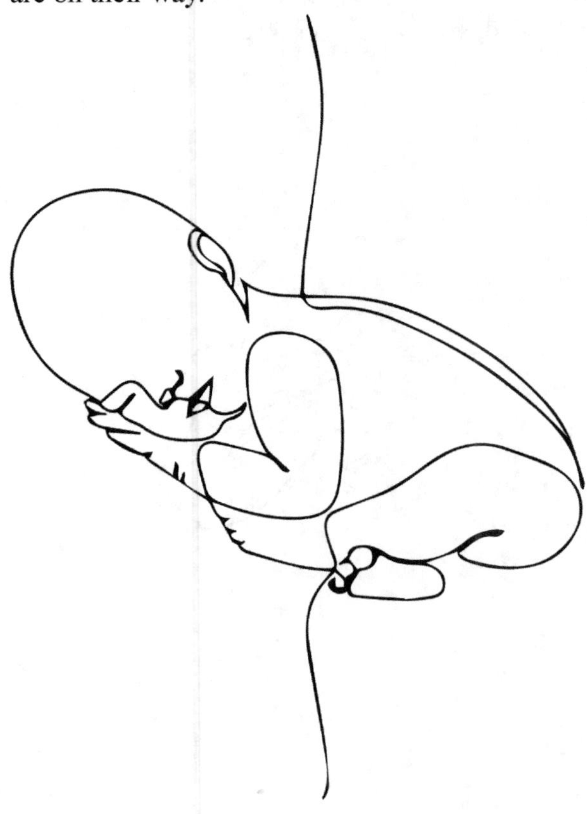

A Moment

You were here for a moment,
The moment was short-lived.
It may have been a moment,
But that moment was a lifetime.

Why does that moment feel like a lifetime?
Probably because it's the greatest gift that you
choose me to be your guardian Angel

Goodnight

I see you
Each and every night
In the moonlit sky
You glow so brightly
You light up the sky with your presence
Each and every night
I look for you
To wish sweet dreams
My angel
May you rest in peace

The Wave Of Emotions

Standing
Cradling
A burst of a wave crashing down

Hard
Tight
A clasp of pain

Despair
Sadness
A path of emptiness

Tears
Heartache
A flood of sorrow

Blankness
Lost
A moment washed away

Angel

Heaven gained an angel
A star has been lit up
You decided this world was not for you
You left behind a broken heart
How I'd be without you
I'm left holding onto the memories

Hole In The Heart

There is a hole in the heart
One that I cannot repair
My heart aches for you
Every moment of every day
My heart calls out for you
Hoping you will hear my cries
My heart drowns in tears
Holding into the precious moments

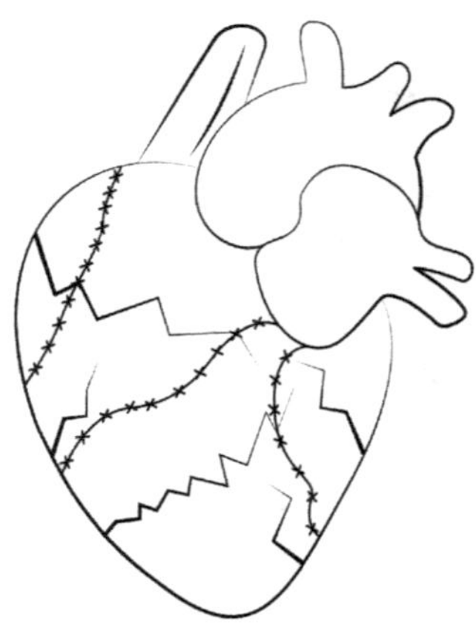

A Dream

Standing there
Clutching my stomach in agony
Fears slowly become reality
One I hoped I won't be facing
A fear that no one would have to endure
Pain, tears and worry
Slowly before I knew it
A dream was being wiped away

Pain

Pain is like a broken glass
Shattered into a million pieces
Pain is like a river
Waves crashing against each other
Pain is like the rainfall
Splattering raindrops on our hearts
Pain is like the stone
Hard to repair from the broken pieces

An Empty Hole

A smile is all it would take to relinquish the
despair,
Nothing would prepare for what was ahead.
Shattered hopes and dreams with broken pieces
of sadness.
All that remains was an empty hole that remains
filled by my angel.

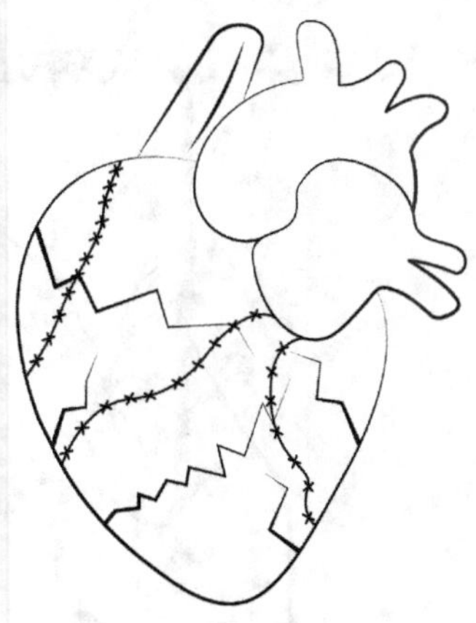

A Walk To Remember

Walking along the beach
Tears in my eyes
Wishing I could have held onto you
You had other plans
You said this world was not for you
So you left behind a broken heart
Shattered into broken pieces

Broken Glass

A road of broken dreams is what lies ahead,
Knowing that you will not be here in my arms.
My heart aches with sadness,
As my arms remain empty of your presence.
You are in a better place now,
Missed everyday and never forgotten.

Lost and Found

It can be found again,
Close your eyes,
Open your heart.
Deep inside your heart,
Lies a beautiful angel.
A special place for the angel,
In the heart.
For the heart is where it shall remain for eternity.

Angel In the Sky

Up above in the moonlit sky,
Shining so brightly,
A star in the horizon,
Shining down.

A glow sparks a firework
Lighting up the sky.
An angel has come,
To bid you good night.

You, Yourself and I

Listen to your heart and you will hear my call,
listen to your soul and you will feel my
presence. I may be gone but I am with you each
and every step of the way.

No matter what hurdles come your way, just
know that every breath is a beating from me to
tell you to keep going.

I am deep within you, I am your strength. I am a
part of you, I am your power. I am with you, I
am your determination to face life no matter
what comes your way.

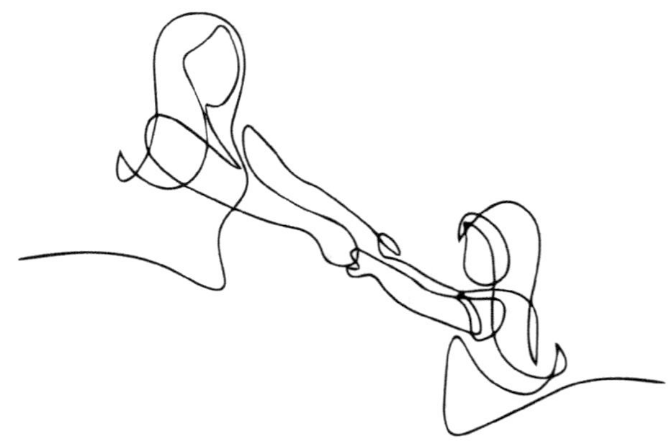

The Void

A lifetime of memories,
Embedded with sadness.
Knowing that there is a void,
Which cannot be filled up.
The pain that once was there,
Remains to be a once upon a time.
No matter how much you try,
Nothing will heal the emptiness that lies behind.

Holding On

As I lay in bed, I am holding onto you, hoping that you are still there somewhere. I'm hoping that you would tell me that you have not left my side, hoping for a miracle that you have heard my calls. I am met with silence as l come to the realisation that you decided that this world was not for you, you decided to go to a better place up above.

I am Yours

It was a privilege
A blessing you choose me
All the moments spent with you
Cherished forever in my heart
Patiently waiting for the day to meet you
Sadly that day never came
Now I'm left with a broken heart
A flood of tears
Unbearable pain knowing that you won't be here
in my arms

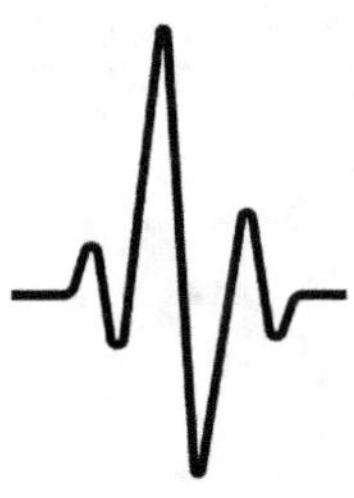

It's Not Goodbye

A goodbye is not a goodbye
It's simply a see you later
As the moon-lit sky lights up
A star that shines so brightly
A star calling out to me
The beautiful angel has arrived
It was never goodbye
The angel returned to answer the call.

Time

As time goes by
There is not a day that goes by
Without thoughts of you.
Little fingers and little toes,
How I longed to hold you in my arms.
Time is the essence of love
Endless love I continue to give you
Grateful to have had this time with you.
My precious little angel

Mummy

My love for you shall never die
My love remains an endless eternal for you
The memories we cherished together
Sealed up tight deep inside my heart
Thankful for the chance to be your Mummy

You may not be here
I will forever be your Mummy
My heart goes on beating for you
The love that is yours
Remains yours for eternity
Thank you for making me a Mummy

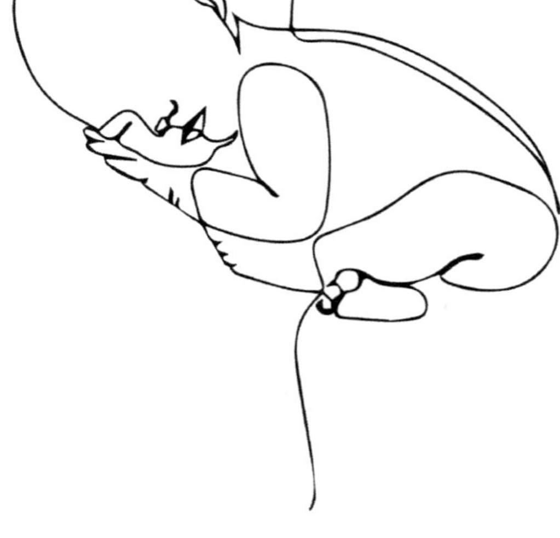